Piano/Vocal + Chord Charts

PLAYBACK+
Speed • Pitch • Balance • Loop

T0061423

Contemporary Worship Classics

To access audio visit:
www.halleonard.com/mylibrary
Enter Code
1068-8126-8877-8429

ISBN 978-1-4950-3463-3

HAL•LEONARD®
CORPORATION

7777 W. BLUEMOUND RD. P.O. BOX 13819 MILWAUKEE, WI 53213

Visit Hal Leonard Online at
www.halleonard.com

www.praisecharts.com

PREFACE

PraiseCharts was started in 1998 by Ryan Dahl, a worship pastor who was striving to develop a team of young musicians, but struggling to find sheet music that kept pace with current trends in music and technology. Today, PraiseCharts has become an invaluable resource for worship leaders around the world, as they tap into a growing online catalog of more than 15,000 worship songs. PraiseCharts is entirely virtual as a company, and yet very personal, practical, tangible and connected. Ryan leads a global team of talented arrangers, transcribers, producers and administrators who desire to make contemporary worship music available to churches worldwide. He lives and works from his home in Langley, British Columbia (Canada), alongside his wife and four children.

PIANO/VOCAL

4	Amazing Grace (My Chains Are Gone)
9	Blessed Be Your Name
23	Forever
14	God of Wonders
30	Here I Am to Worship
34	Holy Is the Lord
46	In Christ Alone
58	Mighty to Save
41	Sing to the King
52	Your Name

CHORD CHARTS

65	Amazing Grace (My Chains Are Gone)
66	Amazing Grace (My Chains Are Gone) (CAPO 1)
67	Amazing Grace (My Chains Are Gone) (CAPO 3)
68	Blessed Be Your Name
69	Blessed Be Your Name (CAPO 2)
70	Forever
72	Forever (CAPO 2)
74	God of Wonders
76	God of Wonders (CAPO 2)
78	Here I Am to Worship
79	Here I Am to Worship (CAPO 1)
80	Holy Is the Lord
82	Holy Is the Lord (CAPO 2)
84	In Christ Alone
86	Mighty to Save
88	Mighty to Save (CAPO 2)
90	Sing to the King
91	Sing to the King (CAPO 1)
92	Your Name
94	Your Name (CAPO 3)

Amazing Grace
(My Chains Are Gone)

Words by John Newton
Traditional American Melody
Additional Words and Music by
Chris Tomlin and Louie Giglio
Arranged by Dan Galbraith

Piano/Vocal
(SAT)

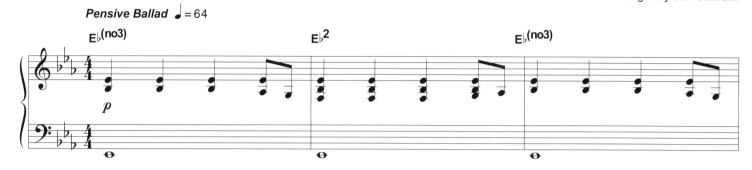

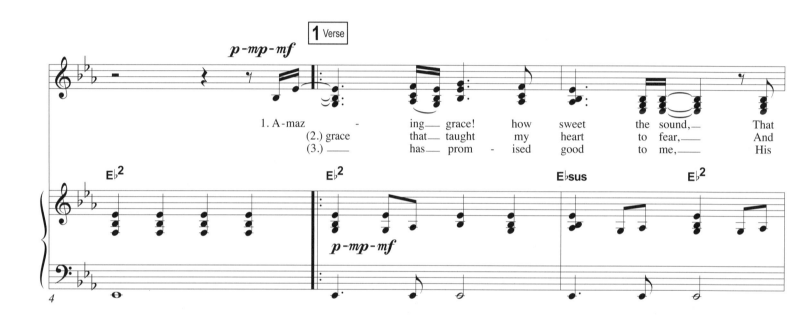

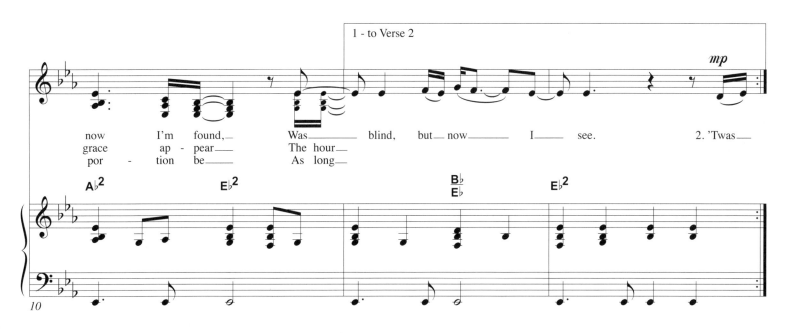

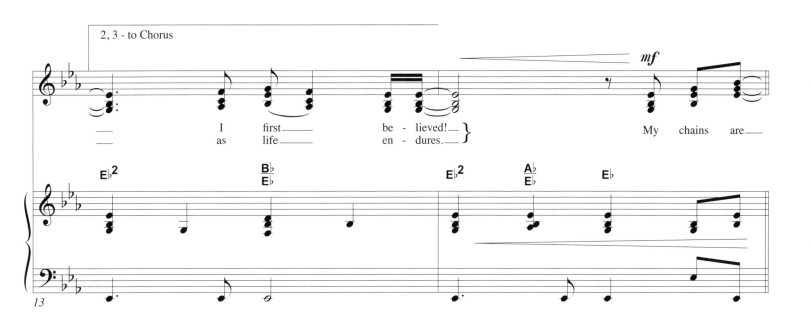

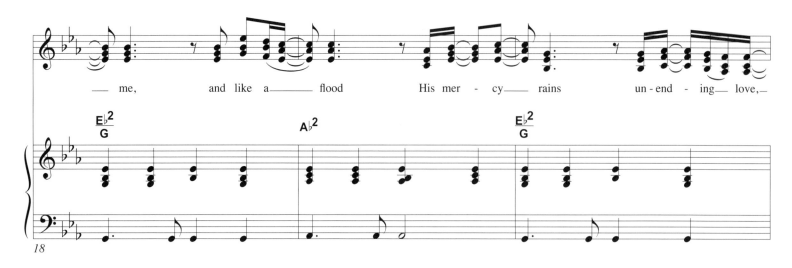

me,   and like a____ flood   His mer - cy____ rains   un - end - ing____ love,____

18

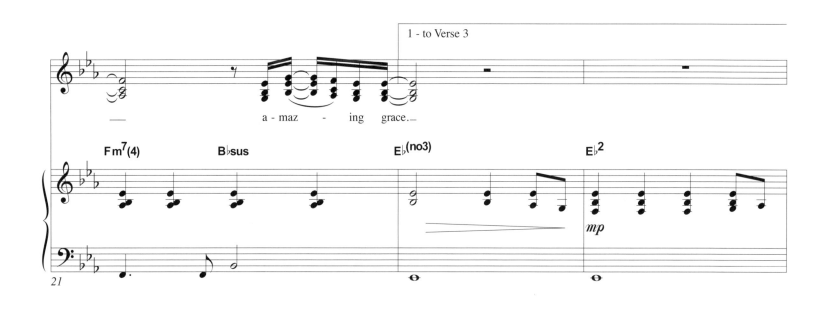

____   a - maz - ing grace.____

1 - to Verse 3

21

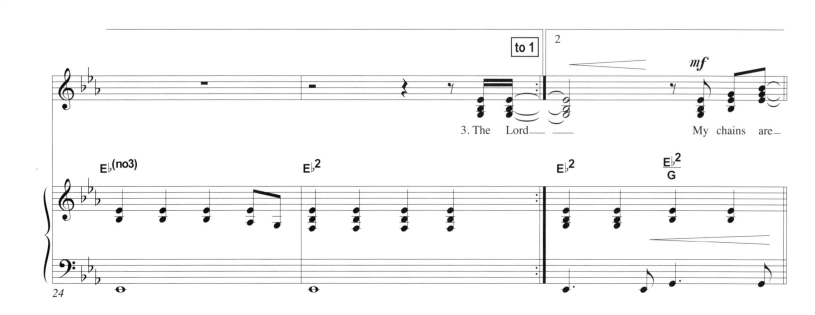

to 1

2

3. The Lord____   ____   My chains are____

24

Blessed Be Your Name

Piano/Vocal
(SAT)

Words and Music by Matt Redman
and Beth Redman
Arranged by Dan Galbraith

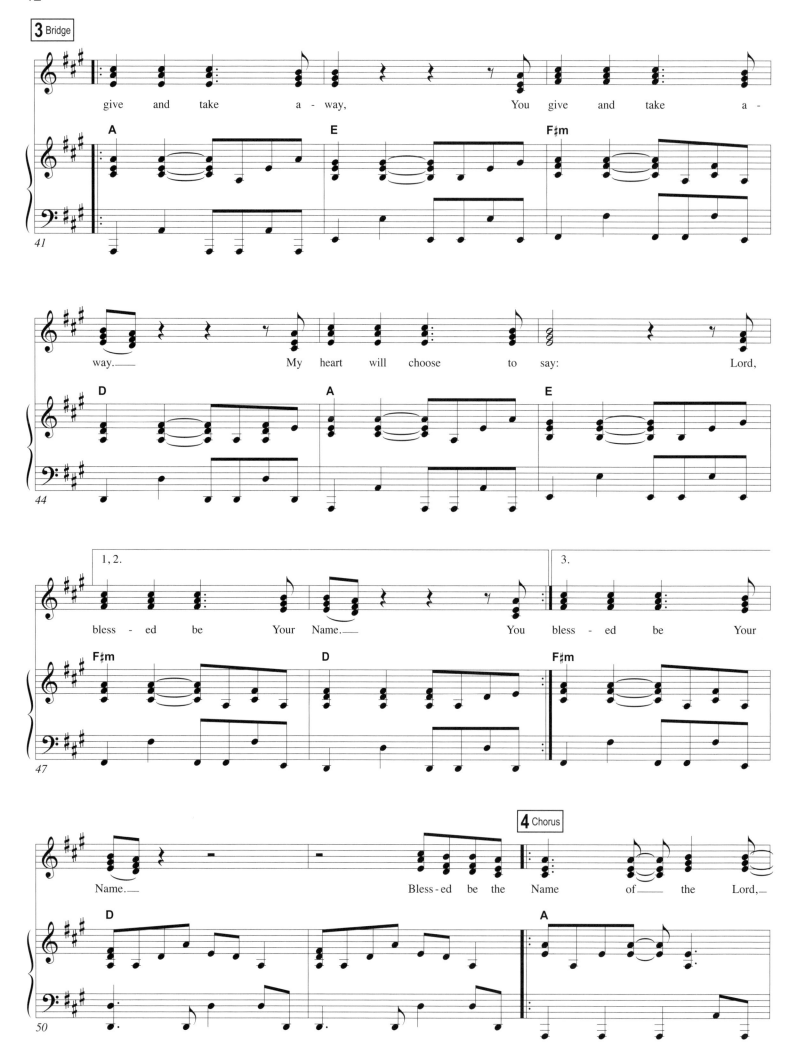

God of Wonders

Piano/Vocal
(SAT)

Words and Music by Marc Byrd
and Steve Hindalong
Arranged by Dan Galbraith

1. Lord of all cre - a - tion,
2. Ear - ly in the morn - ing,

of wat - er, earth, and sky,
I will cel - e - brate the light,

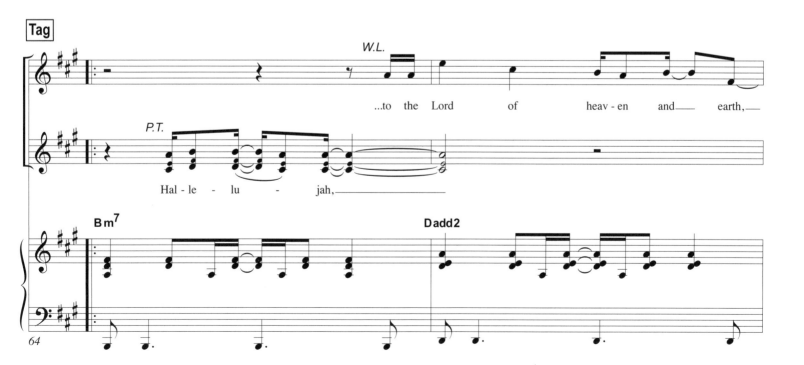

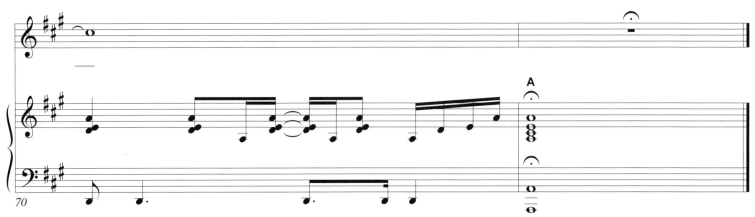

Forever

Piano/Vocal
(SAT)

Words and Music by Chris Tomlin
Arranged by Dan Galbraith

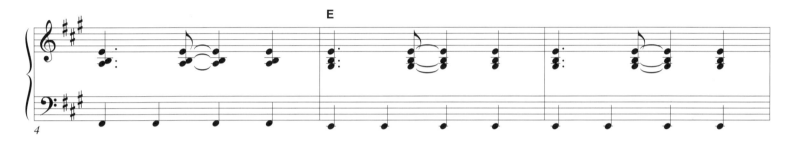

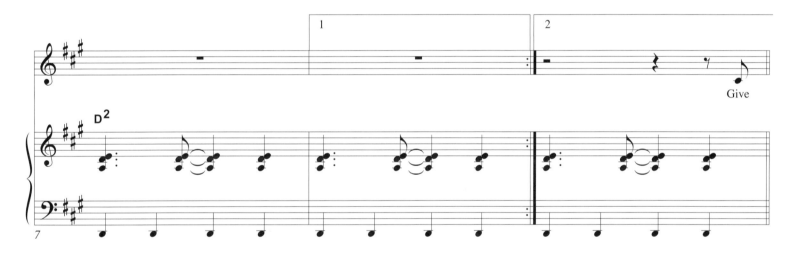

thanks to the Lord,_____ our God and_ King._____ His love en - dures for - ev -

Here I Am to Worship
(Light of the World)

Words and Music by Tim Hughes
Arranged by Dan Galbraith

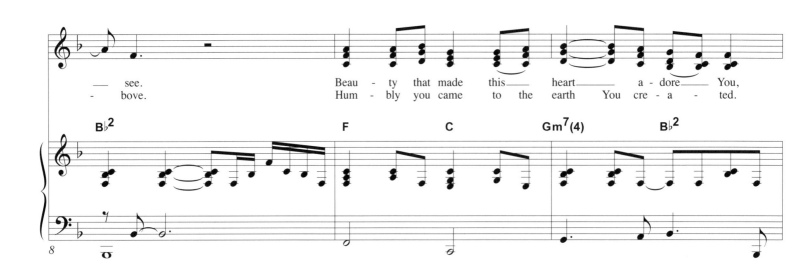

Piano/Vocal
(SAT)

Holy Is the Lord

Words and Music by Chris Tomlin
and Louie Giglio

Arranged by Dan Galbraith

We stand and lift up our hands____ for the joy____ of the Lord____ is our strength.____

____ We bow down____ and wor - ship Him now,____ how great

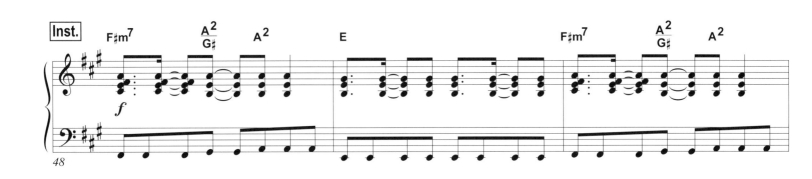

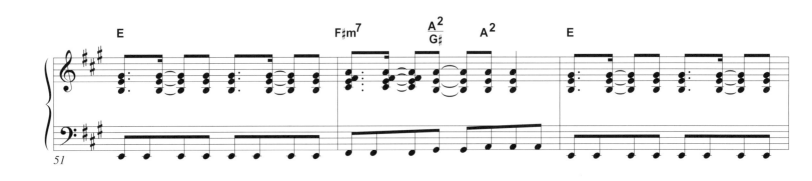

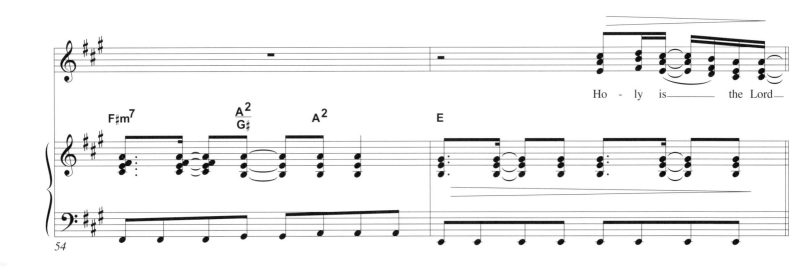

pass

Sing to the King

Piano/Vocal
(SAT)

Words and Music by Billy James Foote
Arranged by Dan Galbraith

Sing to the King Who is com - ing to reign;
For His re - turn - ing we watch and we pray;

Glo - ry to Je - sus, the Lamb that was slain.
We will be read - y the dawn of that day.

Lift up a heart___ of praise;___ Sing now with voic-

-es raised___ to Je - sus;___ Sing to the___

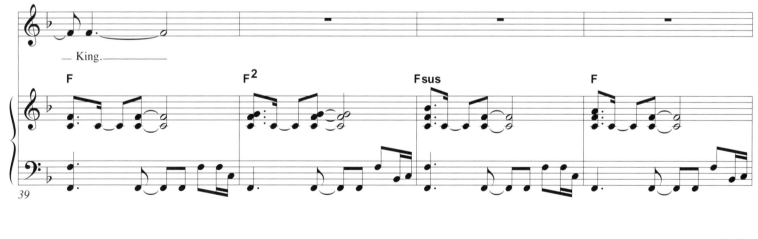

___ King.___

to 1

2nd time D.S. al Coda

CODA

Je - sus___ is King._____ So,

come let us sing___ a song, a song de - clar - ing we

___ be - long___ to Je - sus;___ He is all___ we

___ need.___ Lift up a heart___

In Christ Alone

Piano/Vocal
(SAT)

Words and Music by Keith Getty
and Stuart Townend
Arranged by Dan Galbraith

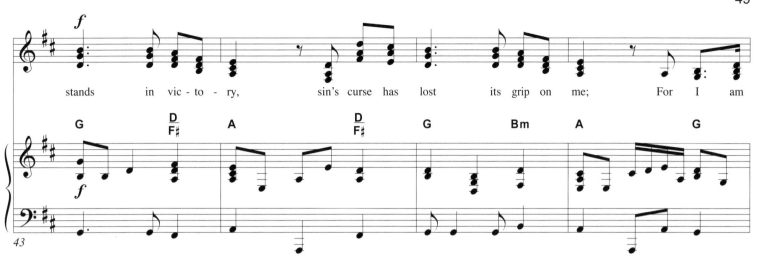

stands in vic-to - ry, sin's curse has lost its grip on me; For I am

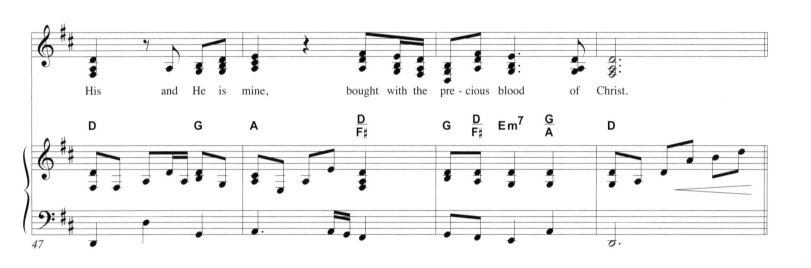

His and He is mine, bought with the pre - cious blood of Christ.

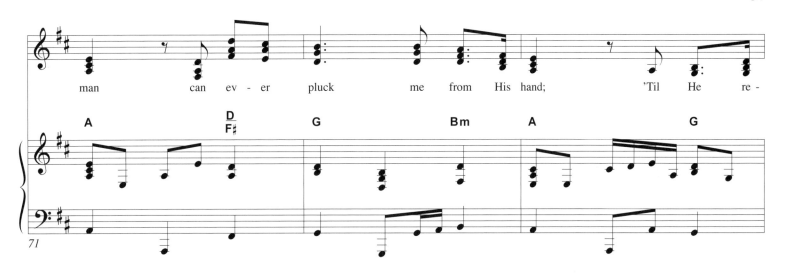

man   can   ev - er   pluck   me   from   His   hand;   'Til   He   re -

turns   or   calls   me   home,   here   in   the   pow'r   of   Christ   I'll   stand.

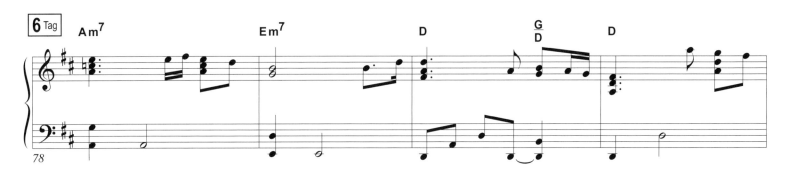

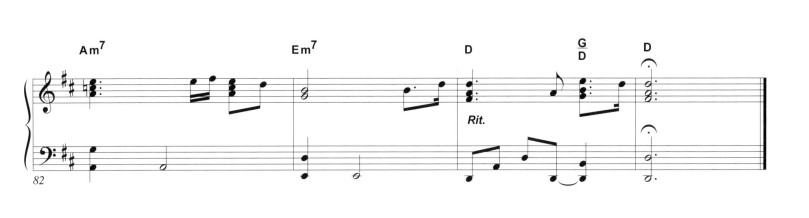

Your Name

Piano/Vocal
(SAT)

Words and Music by Paul Baloche
and Glenn Packiam
Arranged by Dan Galbraith

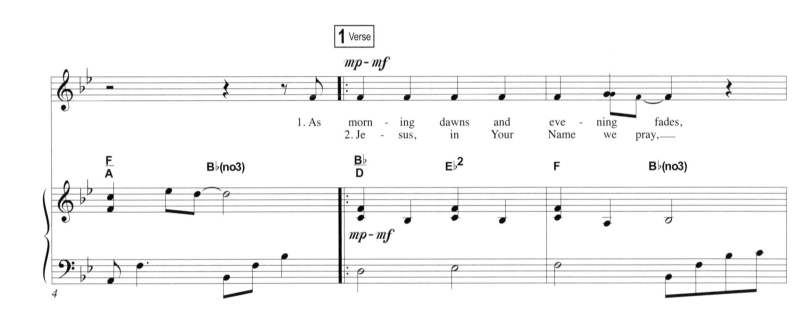

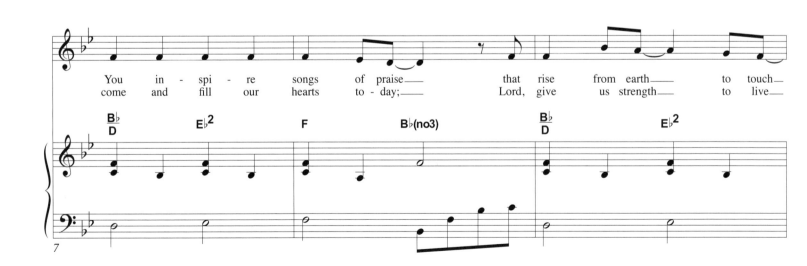

1. As morn-ing dawns and eve-ning fades,
2. Je-sus, in Your Name we pray,

You in-spi-re songs of praise that rise from earth to touch
come and fill our hearts to-day; Lord, give us strength to live

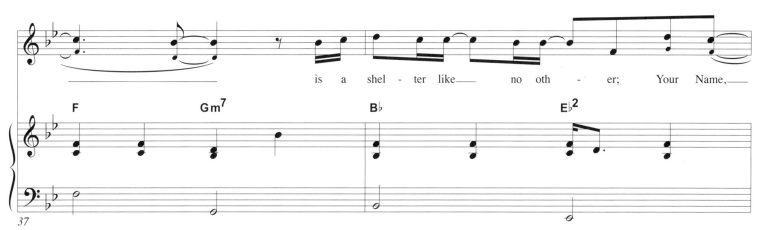

Mighty to Save

Piano/Vocal
(SAT)

Words and Music by Ben Fielding
and Reuben Morgan
Arranged by Dan Galbraith

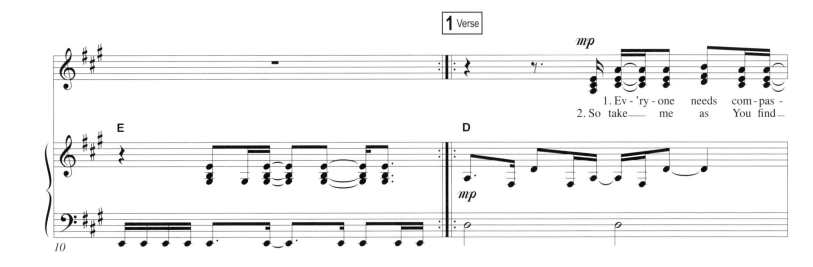

1. Ev-'ry-one needs com-pas-
2. So take___ me as You find___

might-y to save.___ For - ev - er, Au - thor of sal - va - tion, He rose and

con-quered the grave,___ Je - sus con-quered the grave.___

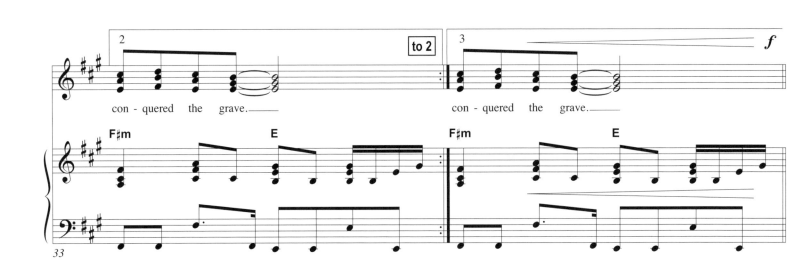

con - quered the grave.___

con - quered the grave.___

Amazing Grace (My Chains Are Gone)

Words by John Newton
Traditional American Melody
Additional Words and Music by Chris Tomlin and Louie Giglio

Key: Eb · Tempo: 62
CCLI Song No. 4768151

Intro (2x)
Eb5 / / / | Eb2 / / /

Verse 1
```
   Eb2                 Ebsus   Eb2                     Bb/Eb
A - mazing grace how sweet the sound that saved a wretch like   me
   Eb2    Eb2/G  Ab2    Eb2                  Bb/Eb Eb2
I once was  lost   but now I'm  found, was blind but  now  I see
```

Verse 2
```
    Eb2                  Ebsus   Eb2                      Bb/Eb
'Twas grace that taught my  heart  to fear and grace my fears re - lieved
    Eb2    Eb2/G   Ab2    Eb2               Bb/Eb     Eb2  Ab/Eb  Eb
How precious   did   that grace ap - pear the hour I   first  be - lieved
```

Chorus
```
            Ab2           Eb2/G         Ab2            Eb2/G
My chains are gone I've been set  free,  my God my Savior has ransomed   me
        Ab2        Eb2/G         Fm7 Bbsus         Eb5
And like a flood His mercy rains    unending  love         amazing grace
```

Intro (2x)

Verse 3
```
   Eb2                 Ebsus   Eb2                    Bb/Eb
The Lord has promised  good  to me, His word my hope se - cures
   Eb2    Eb2/G   Ab2    Eb2               Bb/Eb     Eb2  Ab/Eb  Eb
He will my shield and portion  be  as long as   life   en - dures
```

Chorus (2x)

Verse 4
```
   Eb2                  Ebsus    Eb2                     Bb/Eb
The earth shall soon dis - solve  like snow, the sun forbear to shine
   Eb2    Eb2/G   Ab2    Eb2                Bb/Eb  Eb   Ebsus
But God who called me here be - low will be for -  ever   mine
   Eb2    Bb/Eb  Eb  Ebsus  Eb2    Bb/Eb  Eb2
Will be for - ever  mine You  are for - ever  mine
```

Amazing Grace (My Chains Are Gone) (CAPO 1)

Words by John Newton
Traditional American Melody
Additional Words and Music by Chris Tomlin and Louie Giglio

Key: D · Capo: 1 (Eb) · Tempo: 62
CCLI Song No. 4768151

Intro (2x)

D5 / / / | D2 / / /

Verse 1

```
    D2               Dsus    D2                        A/D
A - mazing grace how sweet the sound that saved a wretch like me
  D2      D2/F#    G2      D2              A/D    D2
I once was  lost  but now I'm  found, was blind but now I see
```

Verse 2

```
     D2              Dsus    D2                        A/D
'Twas grace that taught my heart to fear and grace my fears re - lieved
   D2      D2/F#    G2      D2            A/D     D2    G/D  D
How precious  did   that grace ap - pear the hour I first be - lieved
```

Chorus

```
          G2              D2/F#         G2              D2/F#
My chains are gone I've been set free,  my God my Savior has ransomed   me
          G2        D2/F#        Em7  Asus       D5
And like a flood His mercy rains   unending  love       amazing grace
```

Intro (2x)

Verse 3

```
    D2               Dsus    D2                    A/D
The Lord has promised good to me, His word my hope se - cures
  D2      D2/F#    G2    D2        A/D    D2    G/D  D
He will my shield and portion be as long as life en - dures
```

Chorus (2x)

Verse 4

```
    D2                Dsus    D2                      A/D
The earth shall soon dis - solve like snow, the sun forbear to shine
   D2      D2/F#    G2      D2              A/D   D    Dsus
But God who called me here be - low will be for - ever mine
   D2      A/D  D    Dsus   D2        A/D  D2
Will be for - ever mine You   are for - ever mine
```

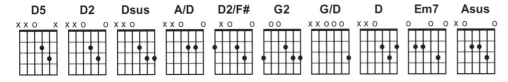

D5   D2   Dsus   A/D   D2/F#   G2   G/D   D   Em7   Asus

Amazing Grace (My Chains Are Gone) (CAPO 3)

Words by John Newton
Traditional American Melody
Additional Words and Music by Chris Tomlin and Louie Giglio

Key: C · Capo: 3 (Eb) · Tempo: 62
CCLI Song No. 4768151

Intro (2x)

C5 / / / | C2 / / /

Verse 1

C2   Csus   C2   G/C
A - mazing grace how sweet the sound that saved a wretch like me
C2   C2/E   F2   C2   G/C C2
I once was lost but now I'm found, was blind but now I see

Verse 2

C2   Csus   C2   G/C
'Twas grace that taught my heart to fear and grace my fears re - lieved
C2   C2/E   F2   C2   G/C   C2   F/C C
How precious did that grace ap - pear the hour I first be - lieved

Chorus

          F2   C2/E   F2   C2/E
My chains are gone I've been set free, my God my Savior has ransomed me
      F2   C2/E   Dm7 Gsus   C5
And like a flood His mercy rains   unending love   amazing grace

Intro (2x)

Verse 3

C2   Csus   C2   G/C
The Lord has promised good to me, His word my hope se - cures
C2   C2/E   F2   C2   G/C   C2 F/C C
He will my shield and portion be as long as life en - dures

Chorus (2x)

Verse 4

C2   Csus   C2   G/C
The earth shall soon dis - solve like snow, the sun forbear to shine
C2   C2/E   F2   C2   G/C C   Csus
But God who called me here be - low will be for - ever mine
C2   G/C C   Csus C2   G/C C2
Will be for - ever mine You are for - ever mine

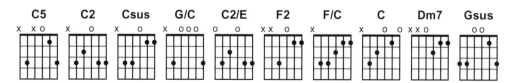

C5   C2   Csus   G/C   C2/E   F2   F/C   C   Dm7   Gsus

Blessed Be Your Name

. . . .

Words and Music by Matt Redman and Beth Redman

Key: A · Tempo: 123
CCLI Song No. 3798438

Intro

A5 / / / | / / / / | / / / / | / / / /

Verse 1

A   E   F#m7   D2

   Blessed be Your name in the land that is plentiful

            A   E   D2

Where Your streams of a - bundance flow, blessed be Your name

A   E   F#m7   D2

   Blessed be Your name when I'm found in the desert place

            A   E   D2

Though I walk through the wilderness, blessed be Your name

Pre-Chorus

A   E   F#m7   D2

   Every blessing You pour out I'll   turn back to praise

A   E   F#m7   D2

   When the darkness closes in Lord,   still I will say

Chorus

            A   E   F#m7   D

Blessed be the name of the Lord, Blessed be Your name

            A   E   F#m7 E   D

Blessed be the name of the Lord, Blessed be Your   glo - rious name

Verse 2

A   E   F#m7   D2

   Blessed be Your name when the sun's shining down on me

            A   E   D2

When the world's all as it should be, blessed be Your name

A   E   F#m7   D

   Blessed be Your name on the road marked with suffering

            A   E   D2

Though there's pain in the offering, blessed be Your name

Pre-Chorus > Chorus (2x)

Bridge (2x)

   A   E   F#m7   D

You give and take a - way, You give and take a -way

   A   E   F#m7   D2

My heart will choose to say Lord blessed be Your name

Chorus (2x) > Intro (2x)

Blessed Be Your Name (CAPO 2)

Words and Music by Matt Redman and Beth Redman

Key: G · Capo: 2 (A) · Tempo: 123
CCLI Song No. 3798438

Intro
G5 / / / | / / / / | / / / / | / / / /

Verse 1
G   D   Em7   C2
   Blessed be Your name in the land that is plentiful
            G   D   C2
Where Your streams of a - bundance flow, blessed be Your name
G   D   Em7   C2
   Blessed be Your name when I'm found in the desert place
           G   D   C2
Though I walk through the wilderness, blessed be Your name

Pre-Chorus
G   D   Em7   C2
   Every blessing You pour out I'll   turn back to praise
G   D   Em7   C2
   When the darkness closes in Lord,   still I will say

Chorus
            G   D   Em7 C
Blessed be the name of the Lord, Blessed be Your name
            G   D   Em7 D   C
Blessed be the name of the Lord, Blessed be Your glo - rious name

Verse 2
G   D   Em7   C2
   Blessed be Your name when the sun's shining down on me
           G   D   C2
When the world's all as it should be, blessed be Your name
G   D   Em7   C
   Blessed be Your name on the road marked with suffering
           G   D   C2
Though there's pain in the offering, blessed be Your name

Pre-Chorus > Chorus (2x)

Bridge (2x)
     G   D   Em7   C
You give and take a - way, You give and take a -way
     G   D   Em7   C2
My heart will choose to say Lord blessed be Your name

Chorus (2x) > Intro (2x)

G5   G   D   Em7   C2   C

Forever

Words and Music by
Chris Tomlin

Key: A · Tempo: 124
CCLI Song No. 3148428

Intro (2x)
A / / / / | / / / / | F#m7 / / / | / / / /
E / / / / | / / / / | D2 / / / / | / / / /

Verse 1
    A2
Give thanks to the Lord our God and King, His love endures forever
D2   **A**
For He is good He is above all things, His love endures for - ever
     E   **D2/F#**
Sing praise, sing praise

Verse 2
A2
    With a mighty hand and outstretched arm, His love endures forever
D2   **A**
    For the life that's been reborn, His love endures for - ever
     E   **D2/F#**   **E**   **D2/F#**
Sing praise, sing praise, sing praise, sing praise

Chorus 1
    A   **F#m7**
For - ever God is faithful, for - ever God is strong
     E   **D2**   **A2**
For - ever God is with us, for - ever for - ever

Verse 3
A2
    From the rising to the setting sun, His love endures forever
     D2   **A**
By the grace of God we will carry on, His love endures for - ever

Pre-Chorus

E	D2/F#	E	D2/F#

Sing praise, sing praise, sing praise, sing praise

Chorus 2

A   F#m7

For - ever God is faithful, for - ever God is strong

E   D2

For - ever God is with us, for - ever, and ever and ever

A   F#m7

For - ever God is faithful, for - ever God is strong

E   D2   A2

For - ever God is with us, for - ever, forever, for - ever

Tag

A2

Give thanks to the Lord for He is good, give thanks to the Lord for He is good

His love endures forever, His love endures forever, His love endures forever

Pre-Chorus

Chorus 3

A   F#m7

For - ever You are faithful, for - ever You are strong

A/E   D2

For - ever You are with us, for - ever

A   F#m7

For - ever You are faithful, for - ever You are strong

A/E   D2   A

For - ever You are with us, for - ever Ooo

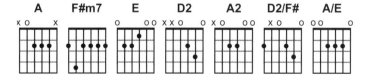

Forever (CAPO 2)

Words and Music by
Chris Tomlin

Key: G · Capo: 2 (A) · Tempo: 124
CCLI Song No. 3148428

Intro (2x)

G / / / | / / / / | Em7 / / / | / / / /
D / / / | / / / / | C2 / / / | / / / /

Verse 1

    G2
Give thanks to the Lord our God and King, His love endures forever
C2   G
For He is good He is above all things, His love endures for - ever
       D   C2/E
Sing praise, sing praise

Verse 2

G2
    With a mighty hand and outstretched arm, His love endures forever
C2   G
    For the life that's been reborn, His love endures for - ever
       D   C2/E   D   C2/E
Sing praise, sing praise, sing praise, sing praise

Chorus 1

    G   Em7
For - ever God is faithful, for - ever God is strong
      D   C2   G2
For - ever God is with us, for - ever for - ever

Verse 3

G2
    From the rising to the setting sun, His love endures forever
      C2   G
By the grace of God we will carry on, His love endures for - ever

Pre-Chorus
```
     D          C2/E        D          C2/E
```
Sing praise, sing praise, sing praise, sing praise

Chorus 2
```
     G                        Em7
```
For - ever God is faithful, for - ever God is strong
```
     D                        C2
```
For - ever God is with us, for - ever, and ever and ever
```
     G                        Em7
```
For - ever God is faithful, for - ever God is strong
```
     D                        C2              G2
```
For - ever God is with us, for - ever, forever, for - ever

Tag
```
G2
```
Give thanks to the Lord for He is good, give thanks to the Lord for He is good

His love endures forever, His love endures forever, His love endures forever

Pre-Chorus

Chorus 3
```
     G                        Em7
```
For - ever You are faithful, for - ever You are strong
```
     G/D                      C2
```
For - ever You are with us, for - ever
```
     G                        Em7
```
For - ever You are faithful, for - ever You are strong
```
     G/D                      C2   G
```
For - ever You are with us, for - ever Ooo

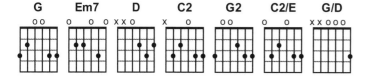

God of Wonders

· ·

Words and Music by Marc Byrd
and Steve Hindalong

Key: A · Tempo: 82
CCLI Song No. 3118757

Intro (2x)
Esus / F#m7 / | D2 / / /

Verse 1
Esus F#m7   D2   Esus   F#m7   D2
    Lord of all cre - ation   of water earth and sky
Esus   F#m7   D2   Esus   F#m7   D2
    The heav - ens are Your tabernacle,   glory to the Lord on high

Chorus 1
A   Esus E   Bm7 D2
God of wonders beyond our galax - y   You are holy holy
    A   Esus E   Bm7 D2
The universe declares Your majes - ty   You are holy holy
D2   E/D   D2   E/D   D2
Lord of heaven and earth, Lord of heaven and earth

Intro (2x)

Verse 2
Esus F#m7   D2   Esus   F#m7   D2
    Early in the morning,   I will celebrate the light
Esus   F#m7   D2   Esus   F#m7   D2
    And when I stumble in the darkness,   I will call Your name by night

Chorus 1

Bridge 1
Bm7   D2   Bm7
    Hallelujah to the Lord of heaven and earth
Bm7   D2   Bm7
    Hallelujah to the Lord of heaven and earth
Bm7   D2   A
    Hallelujah to the Lord of heaven and earth

Instrumental
A / / / | Esus / E / | Bm7 D2
                   Holy holy
A / / / | Esus / E   Bm7 D2
                  Holy Lord

Chorus 2

A   **Esus   E**   **Bm7   D2**

God of wonders beyond our galax -   y   You are holy holy

    A   **Esus   E**   **Bm7   D2**

The universe declares Your majes -   ty   You are holy holy

Bridge 2

A   **Esus**   **Bm7**   **D2**

Precious Lord reveal Your heart to   me, Father hold me hold me

    A   **Esus**   **Bm7   D2**

The universe declares Your majes -   ty   You are holy holy

Chorus 3

A   **Esus   E**   **Bm7   D2**

God of wonders beyond our galax -   y   You are holy holy

    A   **Esus   E**   **Bm7   D2**

The universe declares Your majes -   ty   You are holy holy

      Bm7   Dma9 | / / / / /

You are holy holy

Tag

Bm7   **D2**   **Bm7**

     Hallelujah to the Lord of heaven and earth

Bm7   **D2**   **Bm7**

     Hallelujah to the Lord of heaven and earth

Bm7   **D2**   **Bm7**

     Hallelujah to the Lord of heaven and earth

Bm7   **D2**   **A**

     Hallelujah to the Lord of heaven and earth

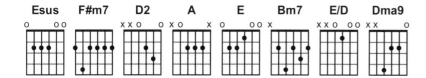

God of Wonders (CAPO 2)

Words and Music by Marc Byrd
and Steve Hindalong

Key: G · Capo: 2 (A) · Tempo: 82
CCLI Song No. 3118757

Intro (2x)
Dsus / **Em7** / | **C2** / / /

Verse 1
Dsus Em7   **C2   Dsus   Em7**   **C2**
     Lord of all cre - ation   of water earth and sky
Dsus   **Em7**   **C2**   **Dsus   Em7**   **C2**
     The heav - ens are Your tabernacle,   glory to the Lord on high

Chorus 1
G   **Dsus   D**   **Am7   C2**
God of wonders beyond our galax -   y   You are holy holy
      G   **Dsus   D**   **Am7   C2**
The universe declares Your majes -   ty   You are holy holy
C2   D/C   **C2**   **D/C**   **C2**
Lord of heaven and earth, Lord of heaven and earth

Intro (2x)

Verse 2
Dsus Em7   **C2**   **Dsus   Em7**   **C2**
     Early in the morning,   I will celebrate the light
Dsus   **Em7**   **C2**   **Dsus   Em7**   **C2**
     And when I stumble in the darkness,   I will call Your name by night

Chorus 1

Bridge 1
Am7   **C2**   **Am7**
     Hallelujah to the Lord of heaven and earth
Am7   **C2**   **Am7**
     Hallelujah to the Lord of heaven and earth
Am7   **C2**   **G**
     Hallelujah to the Lord of heaven and earth

Instrumental
G / / / | **Dsus** / **D** / | **Am7   C2**
                                Holy holy
G / / / | **Dsus** / **D   Am7   C2**
                             Holy Lord

Chorus 2

G   **Dsus D**   **Am7 C2**
God of wonders beyond our galax - y   You are holy holy
   G   **Dsus D**   **Am7 C2**
The universe declares Your majes - ty   You are holy holy

Bridge 2

G   **Dsus**   **Am7**   **C2**
Precious Lord reveal Your heart to   me, Father hold me hold me
   G   **Dsus**   **Am7 C2**
The universe declares Your majes - ty You are holy holy

Chorus 3

G   **Dsus D**   **Am7 C2**
God of wonders beyond our galax - y   You are holy holy
   G   **Dsus D**   **Am7 C2**
The universe declares Your majes - ty   You are holy holy
       Am7 Cma9 | / / / / /
You are holy holy

Tag

Am7   **C2**   **Am7**
   Hallelujah to the Lord of heaven and earth
Am7   **C2**   **Am7**
   Hallelujah to the Lord of heaven and earth
Am7   **C2**   **Am7**
   Hallelujah to the Lord of heaven and earth
Am7   **C2**   **G**
   Hallelujah to the Lord of heaven and earth

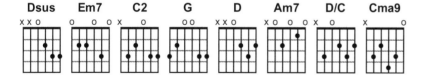

Here I Am to Worship (Light of the World)

· ·

Words and Music by
Tim Hughes

Key: F · Tempo: 76
CCLI Song No. 3266032

Intro
F / C / | Bb2 / / / | F / C / | Bb2 / / /

Verse 1
F   C   Gm7   F   C   Bb2
Light of the world You stepped down into darkness, opened my eyes let me see
F   C   Gm7   F   C   Bb2
Beauty that made this heart adore You, hope of a life spent with You

Chorus
        F   C/E   F/A   Bb2
Here I am to worship here I am to bow down, here I am to say that You're my God
         F   C/E   F/A   Bb2
You're altogether lovely altogether worthy, altogether wonderful to me

Verse 2
F   C   Gm7 F   C   Bb2
King of all days oh so highly exalted, glorious in heaven above
F   C   Gm7   F   C   Bb2
Humbly You came to the earth You created, all for love's sake became poor

Chorus

Bridge (2x)
 C/E F/A   Bb2   C/E   F/A   Bb2
I'll never know how much it cost to see my sin up - on that cross

Chorus > **Bridge** > **Chorus (3x)**

Ending
(Bb2) / / / | / / Csus4 / | Bb2 / / / | / / Csus4 /
Bb2 / / / | / / Csus4 / | Bb2

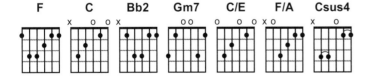

Here I Am to Worship (Light of the World)
(CAPO 1)

Words and Music by
Tim Hughes

Key: E · Capo: 1 (F) · Tempo: 76
CCLI Song No. 3266032

Intro
E / B / | A2 / / / | E / B / | A2 / / /

Verse 1
E   B   F#m7   E   B   A2
Light of the world You stepped down into darkness, opened my eyes let me see
E   B   F#m7   E   B   A2
Beauty that made this heart adore You, hope of a life spent with You

Chorus
        E   B/D#   E/G#   A2
Here I am to worship here I am to bow down, here I am to say that You're my God
        E   B/D#   E/G#   A2
You're altogether lovely altogether worthy, altogether wonderful to me

Verse 2
E   B   F#m7 E   B   A2
King of all days oh so highly exalted, glorious in heaven above
E   B   F#m7   E   B   A2
Humbly You came to the earth You created, all for love's sake became poor

Chorus

Bridge (2x)
 B/D# E/G#   A2   B/D#   E/G#   A2
I'll never know how much it cost to see my sin up - on that cross

Chorus > Bridge > Chorus (3x)

Ending
(A2) / / / | / / Bsus4 / | A2 / / / | / / Bsus4 /
A2 / / / | / / Bsus4 / | A2

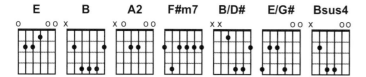

Holy Is the Lord

Words and Music by Chris Tomlin
and Louie Giglio

Key: A · Tempo: 84
CCLI Song No. 4158039

Intro
A5 / D2 / | Esus4 / / / | F#m7 / D2 / | Esus4 / / /

Verse

```
A5              D2      Esus4     F#m7      D2       Esus4
   We stand and lift up our hands, for the  joy  of the Lord is our strength
A5        D2       Esus4             F#m7       D2          Esus4
   We bow down and worship Him now, how great how awesome is   He
                  B    D2          B    D2
And together we sing,     everyone sing
```

Chorus 1

```
          A/C# D2      Esus4     F#m7   D2        Esus4
Holy is the  Lord God Al - mighty, the earth is filled with His  glory
          A/C# D2      Esus4     F#m7   D2        Esus4
Holy is the  Lord God Al - mighty, the earth is filled with His  glory
      F#m7  D2          Esus4
The earth is filled with His  glory
```

Verse > Chorus 1

Bridge

```
    A      E/G#            G6          D
It is rising up   all  around, it's the anthem of the Lord's renown
    A      E/G#            G6          D
It's rising up   all  around, it's the anthem of the Lord's renown
                  B    D2       B    D2
And together we sing,     every - one sing
```

Chorus 1

Instrumental (4x)
F#m7 / A2/G# - A2 | E / / /

Chorus 2

<pre>
            A/C# D2   Esus4   A/C#   D2   Esus4
Holy is the Lord God Al - mighty, the earth is filled with His glory
            A/C# D2   Esus4   A/C#   D2   Esus4
Holy is the Lord God Al - mighty, the earth is filled with His glory
</pre>

Tag

<pre>
Holy is the Lord God Almighty, the earth is filled with His glory
                              A/C#   D2   Esus4
Holy is the Lord God Almighty, the earth is filled with His glory
      A/C#   D2   Esus4   F#m7   D2   E   A2
The earth is filled with His glory, the earth is filled with His glory
</pre>

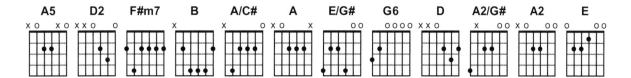

Holy Is the Lord (CAPO 2)

. . . .

Words and Music by Chris Tomlin
and Louie Giglio

Key: G · Capo: 2 (A) · Tempo: 84
CCLI Song No. 4158039

Intro
G5 / C2 / | Dsus4 / / / | Em7 / C2 / | Dsus4 / / /

Verse

```
G5              C2      Dsus4       Em7      C2       Dsus4
   We stand and lift up our hands, for the joy of the Lord is our strength
G5        C2       Dsus4              Em7      C2        Dsus4
   We bow down and worship Him now, how great how awesome is   He
              A   C2          A   C2
And together we sing,     everyone sing
```

Chorus 1

```
            G/B C2    Dsus4       Em7   C2        Dsus4
Holy is the Lord God Al - mighty, the earth is filled with His  glory
            G/B C2    Dsus4       Em7   C2        Dsus4
Holy is the Lord God Al - mighty, the earth is filled with His  glory
      Em7    C2           Dsus4
The earth is filled with His  glory
```

Verse > **Chorus 1**

Bridge

```
   G      D/F#           F6           C
It is rising up  all  around, it's the anthem of the Lord's renown
   G      D/F#           F6           C
It's rising up  all  around, it's the anthem of the Lord's renown
              A    C2        A    C2
And together we sing,     every - one sing
```

Chorus 1

Instrumental (4x)
Em7 / G2/F# - G2 | D / / /

Chorus 2
          G/B C2   Dsus4   G/B   C2   Dsus4
Holy is the Lord God Al - mighty, the earth is filled with His glory
          G/B C2   Dsus4   G/B   C2   Dsus4
Holy is the Lord God Al - mighty, the earth is filled with His glory

Tag
Holy is the Lord God Almighty, the earth is filled with His glory
                                    G/B   C2   Dsus4
Holy is the Lord God Almighty, the earth is filled with His glory
   G/B   C2   Dsus4 Em7 C2   D   G2
The earth is filled with His glory, the earth is filled with His glory

In Christ Alone

Words and Music by Keith Getty
and Stuart Townend

Key: D · Tempo: 62
CCLI Song No. 3350395

Intro (2x)
Am7 / / | Em7 / / | D / G/D | D / /

Verse 1

  G/D   D   G   A   D/F#   G D/F# Em7   G/A   D
In Christ a - lone my hope is found, He is my light my strength   my song

  G   D   G   A   D/F#   G D/F# Em7 G/A   D
This corner - stone this solid ground, firm through the fier - cest drought   and storm

    D/F#   G   Bm7   A   D/F#   G   Bm   A
What heights of love what depths of peace, when fears are stilled when strivings cease

  G   D   G   A D/F#   G D/F# Em7 G/A D   / G/D | D
My Comfort - er my All in all, here in the love   of   Christ   I stand

Verse 2

  G/D   D   G   A   D/F#   G D/F# Em7 G/A   D
In Christ a - lone who took on flesh, fullness of God   in   help   - less babe

   G   D   G   A   D/F#   G D/F# Em7 G/A   D
This gift of love and righteous - ness, scorned by the ones He   came   to save

    D/F#   G   Bm7 A   D/F#   G   Bm   A
Till on that cross as Jesus died, the wrath of God was satis - fied

  G   D   G   A   D/F#   G D/F# Em7 G/A D
For every sin on Him was laid, here in the death   of   Christ   I live

Instrumental 1 (2x)
Am7 / / | Em7 / / | D / G/D | D / /

Verse 3

```
      G/D   D        G    A   D/F#     G    D/F#  Em7  G/A      D
There  in  the ground His body lay, light of the world     by dark  -   ness slain
      G/D   D     G    A   D/F#         G      D/F#  Em7  G/A    D
Then bursting forth in glorious day,  up  from the grave  He   rose      a - gain
      D/F#   G      Bm7   A      D/F#     G     Bm    A
And  as  He stands in victo - ry, sin's curse has lost its grip on me
      G    D    G    A    D/F#        G    D/F#  Em7  G/A    D
For I am His and He is mine, bought with the pre - cious blood      of Christ
```

Instrumental 2

```
Am7 / / |  Em7 / / |  D / G/D |  D / /
Am7 / / |  Em7 / / |  D / G/D |  D / /
Am7 / / |  Em7 / / |  D / G/D |  D / /
Am7 / / |  Em7 / / |  D / / / |  / /
```

Verse 4

```
      G    D    G    A     D/F#      G    D/F#  Em7  G/A  D
No guilt in life no fear in death, this  is the power   of   Christ     in me
      G/D   D    G    A    D/F#        G     D/F#  Em7  G/A    D
From life's first cry to final breath, Jesus com - mands  my   des  -  ti - ny
      D/F#   G      Bm7    A         D/F# G      Bm7     A
No power of hell no scheme of man, can  ever  pluck me from His hand
      G    D    G    A    D/F#       G    D/F#  Em7  G/A    D
Till He re - turns or calls me home, here in the power   of   Christ      I'll stand
```

Instrumental 1 (2x)

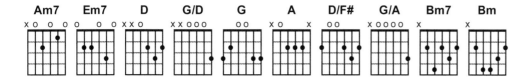

Mighty to Save

Words and Music by Ben Fielding
and Reuben Morgan

Key: A · Tempo: 72
CCLI Song No. 4591782

Intro (3x)
A / / / / | / / / /

Instrumental 1 (2x)
D / / / / | A / / / / | F#m7 / / / / | E / / /

Verse 1
```
D                    A                      F#m7      E
  Everyone needs com - passion, a love that's never failing, let mercy fall on me
D                    A                      F#m7      E
  Everyone needs for - giveness, the kindness of a Saviour, the hope of nations
D / E / | D / E /
```

Chorus
```
A                    E
Saviour He can move the mountains
          D      A     F#m    E
My God is mighty to save, He is mighty to save
       A            E
For - ever Author of sal - vation
            D      A      F#m       E
He rose and conquered the grave, Jesus conquered the grave
```

Instrumental 1

Verse 2
```
D                    A                F#m7   E
  So take me as You find me, all my fears and failures, fill my life again
D                    A                F#m7       E
  I give my life to follow everything I be - lieve in, now I surrender
D / E / | D / E /
```

<u>Chorus (2x)</u>

<u>Instrumental 2</u>
D / A / | E / / F#m | D / A / | E / / F#m

<u>Bridge (2x)</u>
D   A   E   F#m
  Shine Your light and   let the whole world see, we're singing
D   A   E   F#m
  For the glory   of the risen King, Jesus
D   A   E   F#m
  Shine Your light and   let the whole world see, we're singing
D   A   E
  For the glory   of the risen King

<u>Chorus (2x)</u> > **<u>Bridge (3x)</u>**

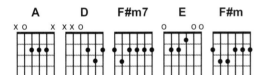

Mighty to Save (CAPO 2)

Words and Music by Ben Fielding
and Reuben Morgan

Key: G · Capo: 2 (A) · Tempo: 72
CCLI Song No. 4591782

Intro (3x)
G / / / / | / / / /

Instrumental 1 (2x)
C / / / / | G / / / / | Em7 / / / / | D / / /

Verse 1
C   G   Em7   D
  Everyone needs com - passion, a love that's never failing, let mercy fall on me
C   G   Em7   D
  Everyone needs for - giveness, the kindness of a Saviour, the hope of nations
C / D / | C / D /

Chorus
G   D
Saviour He can move the mountains
        C   G   Em   D
My God is mighty to save, He is mighty to save
   G   D
For - ever Author of sal - vation
        C   G   Em   D
He rose and conquered the grave, Jesus conquered the grave

Instrumental 1

Verse 2
C   G   Em7   D
  So take me as You find me, all my fears and failures, fill my life again
C   G   Em7   D
  I give my life to follow, everything I be - lieve in, now I surrender
C / D / | C / D /

Chorus (2x)

Instrumental 2
C / G / | D / / Em | C / G / | D / / Em

Bridge (2x)
C   G   D   Em
  Shine Your light and   let the whole world see, we're singing
C   G   D   Em
  For the glory   of the risen King, Jesus
C   G   D   Em
  Shine Your light and   let the whole world see, we're singing
C   G   D
  For the glory   of the risen King

Chorus (2x) > Bridge (3x)

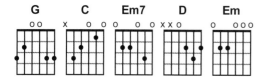

Sing to the King

Words and Music by Billy James Foote

Key: F · Tempo: 122
CCLI Song No. 4010902

Intro (2x)

F / / / / | F2 / / / / | Fsus / / / | F / / /

Verse 1

F   C/F   Bb/F   F   C/F   Bb/F   F

Sing to the King who is coming to reign, glory to Jesus the Lamb that was slain

F   C/E   Bb/D   F/A   Dm7   C   Bb   F

Life and sal - vation His empire shall bring, joy to the nations when Jesus is King

Chorus 1

F   Gm7   Bb   F | Eb2 - Bb /

So come let us sing a song, a song declaring we belong to Jesus, He is all we need

F   Gm7   Bb   C   F

Lift up a heart of praise, sing now with voices raised to Jesus, sing to the King

Intro (2x)

Verse 2

F   C/F   Bb/F   F   C/F   Bb/F   F

For His re - turning we watch and we pray, we will be ready the dawn of that day

F   C/E   Bb/D   F/A   Dm7   C   Bb   F

We'll join in singing with all the re - deemed, Satan is vanquished and Jesus is King

Chorus 1 > **Intro (2x)** > **Verse 2**

Chorus 2

F   Gm7   Bb   F | Eb2 - Bb/D - Bb

So come let us sing a song, a song declaring we belong to Jesus, He is all we need

F   Gm7   Bb   C   F | Eb2 - Bb /

Lift up a heart of praise, sing now with voices raised to Jesus, sing to the King

Chorus 3

F   Gm7   Bb   F | Eb2 - Bb/D - Bb

So come let us sing a song, a song declaring we belong to Jesus, He is all we need

F   Gm7   Bb   C   F

Lift up a heart of praise, sing now with voices raised to Jesus, sing to the King

End

F / / / / | F2 / / / / | Fsus / / / / | F / / /
F / / / / | F2 / / / / | Fsus / / / / | F / / /

F   F2   Fsus   C/F   Bb/F   C/E   Bb/D   F/A   Dm7   C   Bb   Gm7   Eb2

Sing to the King (CAPO 1)

· ·

Words and Music by Billy James Foote

Key: E · Capo: 1 (F) · Tempo: 122
CCLI Song No. 4010902

Intro (2x)
E / / / / | E2 / / / / | Esus / / / / | E / / /

Verse 1
E   B/E   A/E   E   B/E   A/E   E
Sing to the King who is coming to reign, glory to Jesus the Lamb that was slain
E   B/D#   A/C#   E/G# C#m7   B   A   E
Life and sal - vation His empire shall bring, joy to the nations when Jesus is King

Chorus 1
E   F#m7   A   E | D2 - A /
So come let us sing a song, a song declaring we belong to Jesus, He is all we need
E   F#m7   A   B   E
Lift up a heart of praise, sing now with voices raised to Jesus,   sing to the King

Intro (2x)

Verse 2
E   B/E   A/E   E   B/E   A/E   E
For His re - turning we watch and we pray, we will be ready the dawn of that day
E   B/D#   A/C#   E/G# C#m7 B   A   E
We'll join in singing with all the re - deemed, Satan is vanquished and Jesus is King

Chorus 1 > Intro (2x) > Verse 2

Chorus 2
E   F#m7   A   E | D2 - A/C# - A
So come let us sing a song, a song declaring we belong to Jesus, He is all we need
E   F#m7   A   B   E | D2 - A /
Lift up a heart of praise, sing now with voices raised to Jesus,   sing to the King

Chorus 3
E   F#m7   A   E | D2 - A/C# - A
So come let us sing a song, a song declaring we belong to Jesus, He is all we need
E   F#m7   A   B   E
Lift up a heart of praise, sing now with voices raised to Jesus, sing to the King

End
E / / / / | E2 / / / / | Esus / / / / | E / / /
E / / / / | E2 / / / / | Esus / / / / | E / / /

Your Name

Words and Music by Paul Baloche
and Glenn Packiam

Key: Bb · Tempo: 80
CCLI Song No. 4611679

Intro (2x)
Bb/D / Ebma9 / | F/A / Bb5 /

Verse 1

   Bb/D   Eb2   F   Bb5 Bb/D   Eb2 F   Bb5
As morning dawns and evening fades You in - spire songs of praise
   Bb/D   Eb2   F   Gm7   Eb2   F   Bb5
That rise from earth to touch Your heart and glori - fy Your name

Chorus 1

         Dm7 Gm7   Bb   Eb2
Your Name   is a strong and mighty tower
        F   Gm7   Bb   Eb2
Your Name   is a shelter like no other
        F   Gm7   Bb   Eb2
Your Name,   let the nations sing it louder
   Bb/D   Eb2   Fsus F   Bb/D
'Cause nothing has the power to save   but Your Name

Intro

Verse 2

Bb/D Eb2   F   Bb5 Bb/D   Eb2   F   Bb5
Jesus in Your Name we pray, come and fill our hearts to - day
   Bb/D   Eb2   F   Gm7   Eb2 F   Bb5
Lord give us strength to live for You and glori - fy Your Name

Chorus 2

```
          Dm7  Gm7     Bb                    Eb2
Your  Name              is a strong and mighty tower
           F    Gm7     Bb             Eb2
Your Name               is a shelter like no other
           F    Gm7     Bb             Eb2
Your Name,             let the nations sing it louder
       Bb/D           Eb2      Fsus  F           Gm
'Cause nothing has the power to  save    but Your Name
```

Instrumental

```
(Gm) / / / | F / / / | Csus / C / | / / / / |
Gm7 / / / | F / / / | Csus / C / | Eb2 / / / | / / /
```

Chorus 3

```
           F    Gm7     Bb                    Eb2
Your Name               is a strong and mighty tower
           F    Gm7     Bb             Eb2
Your Name               is a shelter like no other
           F    Gm7     Bb             Eb2
Your Name,             let the nations sing it louder
       Bb/D           Eb2      Fsus  F
'Cause nothing has the power to  save    but
```

Chorus 1

Tag (2x)

```
(Bb/D) / Eb2 / | F / Bb5 / |
Bb/D / Eb2 / | F / Bb / | F / Bb /
```

Your Name (CAPO 3)

. . . .

Words and Music by Paul Baloche
and Glenn Packiam

Key: G · Capo: 3 (Bb) · Tempo: 80
CCLI Song No. 4611679

Intro (2x)
G/B / Cma9 / | D/F# / G5 /

Verse 1

| G/B | C2 | D | G5 G/B | C2 | D | G5 |

As morning dawns and evening fades You in - spire songs of praise

| G/B | C2 | D | Em7 | C2 | D | G5 |

That rise from earth to touch Your heart and glori - fy Your name

Chorus 1

| Bm7 | Em7 | G | C2 |

Your Name   is a strong and mighty tower

| D | Em7 | G | C2 |

Your Name   is a shelter like no other

| D | Em7 | G | C2 |

Your Name,   let the nations sing it louder

| G/B | C2 | Dsus D | G/B |

'Cause nothing has the power to save   but Your Name

Intro

Verse 2

| G/B | C2 | D | G5 G/B | C2 | D | G5 |

Jesus in Your Name we pray, come and fill our hearts to - day

| G/B | C2 | D | Em7 | C2 | D | G5 |

Lord give us strength to live for You and glori - fy Your Name

Chorus 2

```
        Bm7  Em7    G                C2
Your  Name          is a strong and mighty tower
        D    Em7    G              C2
Your Name           is a shelter like no other
        D    Em7      G            C2
Your Name,           let the nations sing it louder
    G/B            C2        Dsus  D         Em
'Cause nothing has the power to  save    but Your Name
```

Instrumental

```
(Em) / / / | D / / / | Asus / A / | / / / / |
Em7 / / / | D / / / | Asus / A / | C2 / / / | / / /
```

Chorus 3

```
        D    Em7    G                C2
Your Name           is a strong and mighty tower
        D    Em7    G              C2
Your Name           is a shelter like no other
        D    Em7      G            C2
Your Name,           let the nations sing it louder
    G/B            C2        Dsus  D
'Cause nothing has the power to  save    but
```

Chorus 1

Tag (2x)

```
(G/B) / C2 / | D / G5 / |
G/B / C2 / | D / G / | D / G /
```

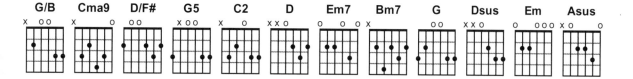

G/B   Cma9   D/F#   G5   C2   D   Em7   Bm7   G   Dsus   Em   Asus

The Best
PRAISE & WORSHIP
Songbooks for Piano

Above All
THE PHILLIP KEVEREN SERIES
15 beautiful praise song piano solo arrangements by Phillip Keveren. Includes: Above All • Agnus Dei • Breathe • Draw Me Close • He Is Exalted • I Stand in Awe • Step by Step • We Fall Down • You Are My King (Amazing Love) • and more.
00311024 Piano Solo...................................$11.95

The Best Praise & Worship Songs Ever
80 all-time favorites: Awesome God • Breathe • Days of Elijah • Here I Am to Worship • I Could Sing of Your Love Forever • Open the Eyes of My Heart • Shout to the Lord • We Bow Down • dozens more.
00311057 P/V/G $22.99

More of the Best Praise & Worship Songs Ever
76 more contemporary worship favorites, including: Beautiful One • Everlasting God • Friend of God • How Great Is Our God • In Christ Alone • Let It Rise • Mighty to Save • Your Grace Is Enough • more.
00311800 P/V/G $24.99

The Big Book of Praise & Worship
Over 50 worship favorites are presented in this popular "Big Book" series collection. Includes: Always • Cornerstone • Forever Reign • I Will Follow • Jesus Paid It All • Lord, I Need You • Mighty to Save • Our God • Stronger • 10,000 Reasons (Bless the Lord) • This Is Amazing Grace • and more.
00140795 P/V/G $22.99

Contemporary Worship Duets
arr. Bill Wolaver
Contains 8 powerful songs carefully arranged by Bill Wolaver as duets for intermediate-level players: Agnus Dei • Be unto Your Name • He Is Exalted • Here I Am to Worship • I Will Rise • The Potter's Hand • Revelation Song • Your Name.
00290593 Piano Duets $10.99

51 Must-Have Modern Worship Hits
A great collection of 51 of today's most popular worship songs, including: Amazed • Better Is One Day • Everyday • Forever • God of Wonders • He Reigns • How Great Is Our God • Offering • Sing to the King • You Are Good • and more.
00311428 P/V/G $22.99

Hillsong Worship Favorites
12 powerful worship songs arranged for piano solo: At the Cross • Came to My Rescue • Desert Song • Forever Reign • Holy Spirit Rain Down • None but Jesus • The Potter's Hand • The Stand • Stronger • and more.
00312522 Piano Solo..................................$12.99

The Best of Passion
Over 40 worship favorites featuring the talents of David Crowder, Matt Redman, Chris Tomlin, and others. Songs include: Always • Awakening • Blessed Be Your Name • Jesus Paid It All • My Heart Is Yours • Our God • 10,000 Reasons (Bless the Lord) • and more.
00101888 P/V/G $19.99

Praise & Worship Duets
THE PHILLIP KEVEREN SERIES
8 worshipful duets by Phillip Keveren: As the Deer • Awesome God • Give Thanks • Great Is the Lord • Lord, I Lift Your Name on High • Shout to the Lord • There Is a Redeemer • We Fall Down.
00311203 Piano Duet................................$11.95

Shout to the Lord!
THE PHILLIP KEVEREN SERIES
14 favorite praise songs, including: As the Deer • El Shaddai • Give Thanks • Great Is the Lord • How Beautiful • More Precious Than Silver • Oh Lord, You're Beautiful • A Shield About Me • Shine, Jesus, Shine • Shout to the Lord • Thy Word • and more.
00310699 Piano Solo $12.95

The Chris Tomlin Collection – 2nd Edition
15 songs from one of the leading artists and composers in Contemporary Christian music, including the favorites: Amazing Grace (My Chains Are Gone) • Holy Is the Lord • How Can I Keep from Singing • How Great Is Our God • Jesus Messiah • Our God • We Fall Down • and more.
00306951 P/V/G $16.99

Top Worship Downloads
20 of today's chart-topping Christian hits, including: Cornerstone • Forever Reign • Great I Am • Here for You • Lord, I Need You • My God • Never Once • One Thing Remains (Your Love Never Fails) • Your Great Name • and more.
00120870 P/V/G $16.99

Worship Together Piano Solo Favorites
A dozen great worship songs tastefully arranged for intermediate piano solo. Includes: Amazing Grace (My Chains Are Gone) • Beautiful Savior (All My Days) • Facedown • The Heart of Worship • How Great Is Our God • and more.
00311477 Piano Solo...............................$12.95

Worship Without Words
arr. Ken Medema
The highly creative Ken Medema has arranged 13 worship songs and classic hymns, perfect for blended worship. Includes: As the Deer • I Could Sing of Your Love Forever • Open the Eyes of My Heart • You Are My All in All • and more.
00311229 Piano Solo...............................$12.95

HAL•LEONARD®
CORPORATION
7777 W. BLUEMOUND RD. P.O. BOX 13819 MILWAUKEE, WI 53213

www.halleonard.com

P/V/G = Piano/Vocal/Guitar Arrangements

Prices, contents, and availability subject to change without notice.

0415